P9-ARN-706

Lettered Creatures

Light Verse by Brad Leithauser

Boston · MMIV

Drawings by Mark Leithauser

David R. Godine · *Publisher*

First published in 2004 by
Davidr. Godine · *Publisher*
Post Office Box 450
Jaffrey, New Hampshire 03452

LIBRARY OF CONGRESS CATALOGING-IN-PUBLICATION DATA

Leithauser, Brad.
Lettered creatures : light verse / by Brad Leithauser ;
drawings by Mark Leithauser. — 1ST ED.
p. cm.
ISBN 1-56792-275-9 (alk. paper) —
ISBN 1-56792-276-7 (special ed. : alk. paper)
1. Animals — Poetry. 2. Alphabet rhymes.
1. Leithauser, Mark, 1950– 11. Title.
PS3562.E4623L48 2004
811'.54—DC22
2004012098

ISBN 1-56792-275-9 (trade edition)
ISBN 1-56792-276-7 (signed limited edition)

First Edition
PRINTED IN CHINA

To
Lance Leithauser
and
Neil Leithauser

For
Two brothers
from
Two brothers

Alphabets: A Greeting

It seems we're each a sort of book —
    As scientists now say —
Composed in the four-letter alphabet
    Of our DNA;
Or call it a book-with-printing-press,
    Since we share the common fate
Of going out of print unless
    We manage to duplicate.
(It appears that Nature's Imperative
    Consists of one rule only: Live.)

So what does it mean — that we are books?
    Perhaps that you and I
(Along with the Mouse, the Moose, the Muskrat,
    Spider and Hangingfly,
The Ground Sloth and the bounding Gazelle,
    The neighbor's ungodly Dog,
Some mite-sized Creature in a shell
    Under a fallen log,
The Eagle and the Bottom Feeder)
    Are each a writer and a reader.

An Anteater

For hole communities,
  Living in buried boroughs, he's
  That nightmare devildoer who
Goes by the name of Clawfoot the Death-Dealing —
  Though from a human point of view
He calls up someone modest and appealing:
Our old round-shouldered grade school janitor,
Forever pushing dust across the floor.

A Beaver

Perhaps because my kind is reared in mud
    And wears a silly, servile grin
The other creatures show me no respect.
Yet I'm earth's leading landscape architect . . .
    They see me differently, it seems,
Only when my expansive plans begin
To rise: putting my smile to work, I flood
Their high-born habitations with my dreams.

Crabs

A sidelong sidling is our gait,
Out here where sea and sun and stone combine.
Our task is to inspect and correlate
Everything the tide leaves.
                              We're searching for some sign,
Some hint, some fresh suggestion . . .
(We're searching for life's meaning — nothing less.)
The answer will come easily, we guess,
Once we locate the question.

Damselfly and Dragonfly

Though fresh as paint, littered with lights,
This pair is old, old as the dinosaurs;
    They buzzed our steaming, teeming shores
When draggling monster-lizards ruled the world —
    As old as those and older still:
    Ancient as days when clanking knights
    Rescued their damsels from the curled
Dragon recluded in the caverned hill.

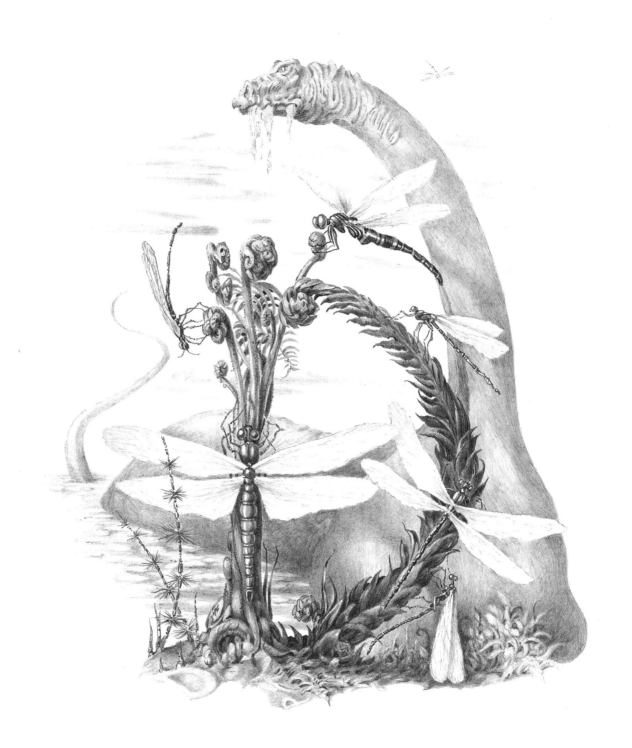

The Emu

The evolution of the flightless bird
Took generations. Having made the skies our own,
We needed aeons to appreciate,
In every hollow bone,
That our forgotten marriage to the earth
Remained solid. Gravity called us and we heard
Its sure, deep-rooted cry. The ground was *good*, and worth
The wait the weight.

A Fly

My little buzz, repeated endlessly,
   Undoes a person's sanity . . .
   The competition's fierce to be
   Earth's Most Annoying Creature, but
   I take the cup —
Or it takes me . . . since Mother Nature specially
   Devised a *plant* with teeth and gut
   To shut me in and shut me up.

Gorillas

You'd like us better if we were more *like* you?
Wore coats and ties? Sported a watch and such?
Or is it otherwise:
                              Are we most fearful/queer
When hints of some near-kinship strike you?
— As when, across the bars of our zoo cell, you peer
Into our mindful eyes and see
Your cousin Gil, who drinks too much,
Or Uncle Frank, in front of his TV.

A Heron

I'm called a *wader*, although given my
      Habit of standing idly by
And just how hard it is to catch my eye,
You may prefer to think of me as *waiter*.
To the fish swimming round me, such distinctions will
      Come to seem striking only later –
Since I'm of no account to them until
      They get the bill.

Iguanas

Under the yellow sun, up out of the blue sea,
Red flames ascended, and fell back.
The flames returned, repeatedly.
The lava hardened, and turned black —
And, as years came and went, grew harder still
And rougher-textured, rucked and torn,
Knobbled and cragged and veined, until
It was more stone than stone, and we were born.

Joey

A baby kangaroo is called a joey.
His early life's a little vertigo-y
Since Mama's always bouncing like a ball.
She doesn't stop to wonder what effect
The bouncing's having on his brain; in fact,
　　　　She doesn't stop at all.
　　　　　　　　kid'll　　　cope?)
　　　(Surely the　　learn to
She's like a kid herself – forever jumping rope.

King Cobras

Our ancestors, keen to invent a
Streamlined existence for themselves, shed through the years
Extraneous impedimenta –
Like arms and legs and ears.
Each of the band became a band,
Or rolled-up tube, where life's necessities were packed:
A few small vials of poison and
A long digestive tract.

Lionfish

The pride of lionfish resides
In our cool, gliding confidence
That there is no conceivable occasion —
No big school dance,
No pirates' feast or pilots' fest,
No fancy ball to benefit the tides,
No Grand Opening of a brand-new ocean —
For which we're underdressed.

A Mantis

Rapt in her layered leaves, lit by an inner light,
She does not stir.
She's dropped into a trance so deep
It looks devout, and, yes,
This *is* religious zeal — though focused less
On providence than provender.
She prays purely for prey: *Don't let me go to sleep*
Hungry tonight.

A Nightingale

A nightingale made a perverse decision:
To live beside a clanging, smoky factory.
She sang, "I now know what it is to be
A lady saloon-singer, offering
Your heart up to a smoking, chatting audience.
Neglected singers have a special mission.
They must sing all the sweeter since
Nobody's listening."

Octopi

Only the outsize net
Of an odd, overwrought vocabulary
Offers the slightest possibility
Of capturing our inky souls — our wary,
Obnubilating getaways, our winding love
Of straitened crevices, the trancing rhythms of
Our oozy otiosity (so weird, and yet
One with the moon-, the sun-, the wind-tossed sea).

Pangolin

Another armored animal?

                       Seems we

    Can never get enough of those

    Whose come-on is a *Go away* . . .

    Why else are we so keen to stay

At the motel whose sign declares, No Vacancy?

        Or fall under the sway

Of one whose dark, reflecting shades disclose

Only our own gaze, yearning helplessly?

Q & A

Q. Those QUILLS of yours – what makes your species so aggressive?
    A. What's your point? *Huh?* We call them "self-expressive."

Q. And your response to those who term you misanthropes?
    A. Talk English, pal. And whya all such dopes?

Q. Do you deny you're prickly? Quick to take offense?
    A. Would you be just as happy with *some* sense?

Q. Returning to those QUILLS – aren't they a trifle cruel?
    A. They're just an ornament – though if some fool . . .

Ruminant

In fragrant, faraway oases, where
    Male camels bent on company repair
For racy chat, it sometimes happens someone can't
    Recall the comely creature who
They're all discussing . . . "But — what *sort* is she?" he'll say.
    And then you'll hear the phrase that will transplant
You to some grimy diner, miles and worlds away:
    "One lump or two?" he asks. "One lump or two?"

Spiders

We run a string
Of small hotels. We're looking to extend
    Our franchise, though we first must find
    A fitting slogan.
                    Rest tonight,
And let us do the rest?
                    We cover everything
You'll ever need?
                    We don't intend
To lose a guest?
                    Relax, while we unwind?
None of them sounds quite right . . .

Turtle

Homebodies? Well, we won't leave home
Without our home – and yet our shell is more
Than shelter from the elements: it's both our ground-
Floor and the vaulted dome
Beneath which is concealed/revealed
The drama of our sex. Our shell is shield
From tooth and claw; and storehouse for
Our food reserves; and, at the close, burial mound.

Striped-Face Unicornfish

Most children learn, regretfully,
There never was an age when unicorns
Grazed the green swales and ridges of the earth.
But things are different in the sea,
Where fluid, fabled dreams are given birth
And unicornfish become reality —
Though they exhibit this peculiarity:
Some have no horns.

Vampire Bats

It's fine, for some, to dine on flowers,
But blood was *meant* to circulate.
We crave a hearty party, with a touch
Of steaming hemoglobin on our plate.
We bear you no ill will; it's not so much
We're tasting as we're toasting you.
Yes – dears – in drinking you, we're drinking to
Your health no less than ours.

Wasps

We're choosy in the company we keep . . .
Our taste runs toward the *raffiné* and bare.
Our homes are one-half paper, one-half air.
There's not a milligram to spare
On our wisp-waisted torsos, though you *will* find there
A little poison pot, since we declare
Most visitors are easier to bear
Once they've been put to sleep.

Exes

X? Spell it ex. As in ex-terminate,
Ex-tinguish, or ex-actly-why-
Were-we-allowed-to-die? The Great
Auk and the Red Gazelle, the Desert Bandicoot,
The Broad-faced Potoroo and Newton's Parakeet,
The Heath Hen, the Bush Wren — they won't
Be coming back. In truth, the Dodo's cry,
Now half lost, was *Don't . . . don't . . .*

Yaks

The light *yackety-yak* of repartee,
The even lighter *yak yak yak* of laughter —
They don't concern us . . . If it's true that we
Likewise long to give voice, you'll learn this only after
You stumble on us huddled in a seething
Three-day blizzard, the mercury thirty below,
Standing like hills of snow on hills of snow . . .
Then you may hear a low snort: *We're still breathing.*

A Zedonk

After Mom had me, it seems I was had.
A foal? A fool — at least they tried to make me one.
　　"Where's Dad?" I used to ask. "Where's Dad?",
　　　Since I alone had none.
　　"He's one of those — those footloose types,"
They said. Or, "He's away. He's working hard . . ."
Working? Or *walking*? In the prison yard.
　　　My dad wears convict's stripes.

Zodiac: A Farewell

The great arc of the zodiac
    Bends like the crown of a tree,
Whose branches house, the Greeks discerned,
    An animal family.
They spied a lion, a crab, a ram,
    Where the Chinese came to see
A monkey, a pig, an ox, a rat . . .
    But if nobody could agree
On anything's identity,
Neither side lacked for company.

The great ark of the zodiac
    Is adrift on an endless sea.
There's comfort in knowing its cargo can come
    To no harm from you and me,
That no storm of human contriving could
    Ever reach so far . . .
The constellations' great consolations
    Lie there: in how distant they are,
And how bright the way they, high and dry,
Shelter in the open sky.

AUTHOR'S NOTE

Respectable as most of them may look, a number of these creatures turn out to be kleptoparasites. The Pangolin has pilfered half a line from Marianne Moore, and the Emu has lifted an entire line from one of my favorite lettered creatures, Richard Kenney. Other thefts may reveal themselves in time . . .

"Alphabets: A Greeting" is dedicated to Ann Close; the Anteater to Jón Karl Helgason and Frída Jónsdóttir; the Beaver to David Mohney; the Crabs to those sometime Cape Codders Cynthia Zarin and Joseph Goddu; the Damselfly/Dragonfly combination to Glyn and Geraldine Maxwell; the Emu to Peggy O'Shea; the Heron to Deborah Gelstein Page; the Iguanas to the memory of Dr. David Sigelman; the Joey to Joan Abrahamson; the Lionfish to Holly Brubach; the Mantis to Phil DeVries; the Nightingale to Brock Walsh and Joy Horowitz; the Octopi to Anthony and Helen Hecht; the Pangolin to Pengyew Chin; the Ruminant to Arthur Higbee; the Striped-face Unicornfish to Cornell Fleischer; the Yaks to Sigurdur G. Tómasson and Steinunn Bergsteinsdóttir, in whose summerhouse the series was completed; the Zedonk to Daniel Hall; and "Zodiac: A Farewell" to Christopher Carduff.

ARTIST'S NOTE

"Why not an alphabet book?" she asked, a question finally answered decades later. The book's first drawing, "Lettered Creatures," is dedicated to my resolute mother, Gladys Leithauser.

The Heron drawing is dedicated to Jim and Rosemarie Howe, in whose creek-side home these creatures first began to appear; the Lionfish to Anthony Hecht; the Fly to the memory of Frances Smyth; the Crabs to Linda Pastan; the Iguanas to Paul Richard; the Exes to Dodge Thompson; the Zodiac to Margaret and Francis O'Neill; the Octopi to Ken and Marilou Hakuta; the Damselfly/Dragonfly combination to Susan Arensberg and Neal Turtell; the Nightingale to Mary Jo Salter; the Wasps to Bryan and our friend Will "the Honeybee" Billow; the Mantis to Anna; the Vampire Bats to Hamilton, Walter and Harry, true creatures of the night; and the Joey to Henry, George and Logan, three with twenty-six to learn.

ABOUT THE AUTHOR

BRAD LEITHAUSER was born in Detroit in 1953 and graduated from Harvard College and Harvard Law School. He is the author of four previous volumes of poetry — *Hundreds of Fireflies*, *Cats of the Temple*, *The Mail from Anywhere*, and *The Odd Last Thing She Did* — and a novel in verse, *Darlington's Fall*. He has also published five other novels and a book of essays, and edited *The Norton Book of Ghost Stories* and *No Other Book: Selected Essays of Randall Jarrell*. He is the recipient of many awards for his writing, including a Guggenheim Fellowship, an Ingram Merrill grant, and a MacArthur Fellowship. An Emily Dickinson Senior Lecturer in the Humanities at Mount Holyoke College, he lives with his wife, the poet Mary Jo Salter, and their two daughters, Emily and Hilary, in Amherst, Massachusetts.

ABOUT THE ARTIST

MARK LEITHAUSER was born in Detroit in 1950. He received a bachelor's degree in the classics and two master's degrees in the fine arts from Wayne State University, where he taught studio art. Since 1973, he has exhibited his etchings, drawings, and paintings in solo and group shows at the Coe Kerr Gallery, the Brooklyn Museum, the Corcoran Gallery of Art, the Library of Congress, the Chrysler Museum, and the Museum of American Art, and he is currently represented by the Hollis Taggart Gallery in New York City. He previously collaborated with his brother Brad by creating woodcuts for the chapbook *A Seaside Mountain* and twelve pencil drawings for *Darlington's Fall*. A senior curator and the chief of design at the National Gallery of Art, he lives with his wife, Bryan, and their two children, Hamilton and Anna, in Washington, D.C.

COLOPHON

LETTERED CREATURES has been set in digital versions of Bruce Rogers's Centaur and Frederic Warde's Arrighi. Among the numerous revivals of the types of Nicolas Jenson, Centaur is arguably the most elegant interpretation of the type used by Jenson in his widely admired 1470 edition of Eusebius's *De Præparatione Evangelica*. Eager to maintain the spirit and proportions of his model, Rogers drew his letters directly on enlargements of Jenson's printed letters with a minimum of retouching. The result was a face of more distinct calligraphic emphasis and livelier letterforms than other Jenson revivals. Its bracketed serifs give it an aristocratic bearing that its cousins — among them the Kelmscott Press's Golden type and the Doves Press type — lack. ⋮ Commissioned as a proprietary face for the Metropolitan Museum of Art in New York, Centaur was licensed to the Monotype Corporation in 1929. Faced with the problem of creating an italic to accompany the roman — a feat he did not feel qualified to attempt — Rogers turned to Warde to fill the gap. Modeled upon a chancery italic cut in 1527 by Ludovico degli Arrighi, the resulting type has an easy rhythm and gracious letterforms that admirably complement Rogers's roman.

Design & composition by Carl W. Scarbrough

◆　◆　◆